KINGFISHER
BLUES

KINGFISHER BLUES

POEMS

ERIK REECE

FIRESIDE
INDUSTRIES

Published by Fireside Industries
An imprint of the University Press of Kentucky

Editorial and Sales Offices: The University Press of Kentucky
663 South Limestone Street, Lexington, Kentucky 40508-4008
www.kentuckypress.com

Library of Congress Cataloging-in-Publication Data

Names: Reece, Erik, author.
Title: Kingfisher blues : poems / Erik Reece.
Description: Lexington, Kentucky : Fireside Industries, 2024.
Identifiers: LCCN 2024026129 | ISBN 9781950564491 (hardcover) | ISBN
    9781950564507 (paperback) | ISBN 9781950564514 (pdf) | ISBN
    9781950564521 (epub)
Subjects: LCGFT: Poetry.
Classification: LCC PS3551.N4123 K56 2024 | DDC 811/.54—dc23/eng/20240627
LC record available at https://lccn.loc.gov/2024026129

for Melissa
who saw me through

isolate a grammar
unleashed
from fear

—MAXINE CHERNOFF

Contents

*   *   *

I

The Story of a County Jail

The sign on the wall inside the county jail
forbade men and women from making eye contact.
From a bank of phones beneath the sign, I heard
a woman say, "Honey, this is no time for questions.
Just bring my stripper boots when you come."
After they cut the rest of us loose in the morning,
a guy walking out beside me pointed across
to the new jail still under construction and said,
"I swear I'm never gonna end up in that place."
And I thought, *He's right: what's needed here*
are clear goals, some good orderly direction.
I tried to amuse Melissa with what had transpired
while she was down at the courthouse, trying to
go my bail. But all she said was, "Let's not pretend
you're some kind of Henry David Thoreau,
regaling the world with your night-in-jail story."
She was right as well. The Concord constable
didn't arrest old abstemious Henry for bellowing
out "Midnight Confessions" while he drunkenly
made snow angels in a neighbor's front yard.
"I can't help it," I said. "For some weird reason
whenever I drink, I break out in handcuffs."
"I'm glad you find this all so funny," Melissa said,
and because of the catch in her voice, I decided
not to ask if she remembered my stripper boots.

Luna Moths

Tonight I found eight luna moths pressed against our screen
  door.

It was a green glory, perhaps an incidental omen.

I keep thinking I should try to gather again
all the friends I've scattered through foolish negligence.

I used to imagine it somehow heroic to be a woodland recluse
until that honest disposition turned into this chemical
  retreat,

with me hiding under the pale leaf of a shagbark hickory.

Who said these dying moths are a symbol of rebirth?
Probably the same person pouring found vodka down the
  sink.

Probably the same person
telling me this pose
                    isn't pretty anymore.

Hazard

I woke this morning thinking about an old friend in Hazard,
how we used to drink beer on a stone wall above that city,
talking until dark about Springsteen and the failures of our
    fathers.

I was going to call and remind him of all that until
I finally shook off sleep and remembered that he's dead.

Once when we were all flying high on good mezcal,
his wife crashed drunk into my lap at the dinner table.

The chair shattered, and we collapsed into a sprawling
convolution of tangled limbs and idiotic laughter.

An unexpected kiss followed, and then things got
difficult. My friend pretended he didn't mind at first,

and then he pretended that we weren't friends.
In the end, he even pretended he was dead,
the same way I'm pretending to be alive.

Driving Montana

Ponderosa logs are stacked high and wide on the flatbed in
   front of me
because I'm driving with the ghost of Richard Hugo across
   northwest Montana.

At Johnson's Café outside East Glacier,
there's a cowboy manikin stuffed inside a phone booth,
like the lonesome embodiment of a Hank Williams song.

And there's a cook who will show you the claw marks
a grizzly left on his back just before he shot it.

The Two Medicine River creeps quietly past.

As for me, I put my life back East on hold and lost a paycheck
at the Blackfeet casino in Browning.
                                   No matter.

I can press my luck up against the Front Range
and scatter magpies at eighty miles an hour.

Clouds pool in shallow coulees,
and the river throws off the sun just like it always does.

This prairie shorn of its tall grass in the early fall
still looks like the surface of the sea,
fished from above by diving falcons.

Nothing back East prepares you for driving out here,
the way everything just sweeps away toward the edges,
and antelope up on the butte still flee
jaguars that went extinct a thousand years ago.

"Who wants a Ranier beer?" says Hugo,
reaching for the cooler.
                              I do; I surely do.

All this God talk on the radio is getting me down.
Can't we just have some bad local news or a decent Link Wray
    rip-off?

I think about the monks back home at Gethsemani,
never ranging further than the sound of bells calling them to
    their offices.

But maybe this movement can be a kind of meditation,
counting miles like counting breaths,
each a path to a never-arriving horizon,
and so a path that is really only a presence.

"You know," says Hugo, "a good day driving in Montana
is like a woman who loves you."
                              That seems right to me.

There is a woman who loves me and
whom I could compare to this day:
open, forgiving, good company. But she's not here,

and the Blackfeet warriors who hunted the blackhorn bison
are also gone,
                    while the old poet wanders off
to translate the scarlet dreams of five cutthroat trout.

Now, it's just me out driving this long empty road,
with the Rockies on my right
and my own ghosts
stampeding in from the East,
                                        trying to track me down.

Black Veil

Prince Lorca, Courtier Vallejo, Minister Neruda:
I never understood your Spanish fascination with death
until it crept into my own entrails and encamped there,
like assassins digging a potter's field at Fuente Grande.
Except I was the assassin and my body a thing to be flung
in that mass grave where addicts are always piling up.

In one year, three friends died of the drink, and I too
could see inside my own glass, the moon setting with a tomb-
stone in its throat. But I went on boozing because, after all,
I wasn't dead, and the coffins already under black sails
hadn't yet found this riverbank. Still I kept a careful eye
on the urn with its throat cut and listened hard

to the strange voices emanating from inside. But they kept
getting drowned by the frantic cry of a man who is forever
losing his dog and rides these roads calling, calling.
It's only the paper-mache mask, plastered together
with pages from local obituaries, that never speaks.
Still it's sad to read in those lines all the lives distilled

down to a hundred words, some of them no doubt true.
When I leave the mask out in the rain, carrion come to
drink from its dead eyes. My father was a country preacher,
and when I remember his violent end, I sometimes think

of the parable about a minister who wore a black veil
all his life and even refused to remove it on his deathbed

when huddled parishioners begged to see his face at last.
"I look around me, and lo! on every visage a black veil!" he
    cried
out in one final breath. My father's death was not so symbolic,
but still we struggled to comprehend his swift departure.
Now my mother pleads with me to end what seems to her
another suicidal spiral around the double helix that has
    always

cursed our family. Is there no absolution for these sins
of the father and those of his only son? Didn't we paint a cross
of blood above our very door? Lorca, Vallejo, Neruda:
the agents of death could not abide how you hunted down life
with such ardor and purpose. Please show me a sign
that this curse might be lifted and this veil finally dropped.

Nuptials

We were married down beside Clear Creek
on a flat slab of limestone big enough to hold
you and me, the preacher, and two witnesses.
One of them took our picture, and the other baked
us an apple cake drizzled in caramel and bourbon.

You wore hiking boots under your wedding dress.
The ginkgo trees blazed like the gates of Eden.
We drank Dom Pérignon for the first time
in our lives because the realtor had given us a bottle.
We would be happy here; who could doubt it?

Ten years later you are ransacking the house and
digging through drawers for any sign of booze.
We scream vile accusations at each other.
All the bird songs I memorized have gone silent.
The oaks stand sentry over our desperation.

Once I told you these woods were so beautiful,
a man needed nothing else to make him happy.
And once I told you my only happiness would
mean drinking myself to death in these woods.
Those still seem to me the only real options.

Middle ground is gone. A choice must be made.
The leaning oaks await an answer. Leopard moths

press against the screen like children who've
been sent outside so their parents can fight.
"Please come back to me," is what you said.

The River

I don't trust a man that doesn't drink.

—BIG MOMMA, *CAT ON A HOT TIN ROOF*

My dogs are great enablers because they know
a woman at the liquor store will be ready with a treat
when I pull up to the drive-through at ten this morning.
"Who wants a milk bone?" she'll ask in her dog voice,
before handing a bottle over to the boozehound.
From there, it's only a ten-minute drive to the river,
where the canines scout the bank with genetic zeal.
"Nobody knows we're here," I grandly announce,
and my companions look up, as if this secret
is a sudden burden they didn't expect to bear.
I dig my ancient camp cup into a bag of ice,
then fill it with what Jim Harrison rightly called
that faux elixir (otherwise known as Polish vodka).
A pair of kingfishers sweep low across the water,
hurling down at me their usual shrill invective.
Vultures circle ominously above the palisades,
but I've long grown used to that death spiral.
Right now, I should be sitting in my doctor's office,
trying to register the severity of my blood tests
while he repeats his annual, "If you keep this up . . ."
Does he mean the vultures will descend to feast
on my liver? I think that's exactly what he means.
So I ask, "Who has time for such foreboding when
the sun is starting to crest over limestone bluffs
right before it shatters across the river's surface?"

The ethanol now pumping through my veins
has accomplished once more a chemical alchemy
that dissolves past and future dread into this
alcoholic present where cautionary tales
can't find me. To live here too long is to die,
I know, and some would call this a kind of death,
but that's only a view from above, a vulture's
perspective or a Roman Stoic's, while here
behind my eyes, a great calm is washing around
my limbic lobe, something like the *click* Brick heard
in his own head to make Big Daddy disappear.
That click can't last, but it has to work at least until
I shed this skin and dive into the dark forget-
fulness where northern drum brush my bones
with their purple fins and speak in phrases
of our common ancestor. In that early paradise,
self was no subject to sabotage. Our exile was far
in the future, and our fears hadn't yet flung us up
on these shoals like ten thousand sanderlings
untethered from what once had made us whole.

Show's Over

The wooden horses finally broke free from the derelict
carousel.
They galloped through high grass, then climbed into the
northern sky
to join once more the spiral galaxy inside their ancestral
constellation.

When the horses were gone, I stood alone under those distant
suns,
my company a mute congregation of dangling drive-in
speakers.

Who knows where to look for all the lost fathers?
The one riding next to me on the carousel disappeared
soon after the carnival left town.

> All we found in the attic
> were large hearts made from
> chicken wire—
> rusted cages full of rags
> still dripping with gasoline.

Myself When I Am Real

I used barbed wire to restring the upright bass,
and with bleeding fingers on shaking hands,
plucked out all my favorite songs of self-pity.

I folded back the horseshoe crab's hind carapace
and slowly extracted all that pure, blue blood
to sweep clean the needles dancing under my skin.

Remember the Bristol Boom-Boom Room
where chilled vodka flowed through the veins
of a Venus de Milo ice sculpture, then spilled

from her cold nipples into my anxious mouth?
Did anyone notice how at midnight my head
somehow broke through her frozen uterus,

then rolled across the floor to your kick drum?
You picked it up and yelled into my melting face,
"I don't know who you are any more," then added,

"It's like I'm living with a complete fiction."
On muscle memory alone, my headless body
tried again to reprise "Myself When I Am Real,"

a minor, but pretty fantastic Mingus number.
Even you paused to consider my sincerity,
to wonder if you'd be a fool believing in me

one more time. I thought I even saw a smile
when you placed my head up on the spike
of your high hat, like a cup of trembling.

Then, with brushes barely sweeping the cymbals,
you tried to coax me out of this long, looping solo
and into a new terrain, a different tune,

something like that.

The Last Chance Liquor Store

My Palestinian neighbor kneels on a prayer rug
in the corner of his county-line liquor store.

I quietly lift a bottle of Tito's from the shelf,
leave a twenty next to the register,

and drive off thinking,
>   Is this the last day I might get away
>   with lying to Melissa?
>   That's what I was thinking.

Back at the gas company
I had an older supervisor
who hid bottles of cheap vodka all around the plant.

He was close to retirement, so everyone else pretended not to
    notice.
But in the arrogance of youth, I thought him pathetic.

Now I don't feel so self-righteous.
Now I understand him quite plainly.

I understand how a man can slip
from confidence and competence
Into asking, "How can I just make it through this day

       unnoticed,
       unsuspected,
       unredeemed?"

Loner

When I was a kid, other children terrified me.
I just wanted to be left alone to draw, or kick
my football over the backyard clothesline, or
make a foxhole under my mother's old coats.
A cedar chest sat in our basement. It held
my grandmother's quilts and my dead father's
vestments. When I placed his red stole around
my neck, the gold fringe touched my feet. So
I stretched out inside the trunk and pulled
the lid shut. The smell of cedar filled my head.
That dark quiet felt like the world's oldest
and smallest church. I was a congregation of one.

The Marcus Aurelius Motel

Flood-ruined carpets pile up around the dumpster
and their stench drifts into my cheap motel room,
which happens to be heaven right now because
there's no one to tell me, "That's your last drink."

The man I pay to hear me talk says, "Drinking alone
in a motel isn't most people's idea of a good time,"
and it's like he speaks a language I almost understand;
it's like he's from a country I can't find on the map.

I never got so desperate that I cracked a green bible
while entertaining myself in those dank little rooms.
That's strictly the story of some low-bottom drunk.
No, I always brought my Marcus Aurelius along

just in case the notion struck me to change my life.
"What stands in the way becomes the way," Marcus wrote
in his tent while commanding troops along the Danube.
I text that to someone who doesn't want to hear it anymore.

Melissa used to think it cute how I always asked
for a room near the ice maker. But that was early on.
I was still joking and quoting famous Churchill lines
whenever someone questioned my seventh drink.

Listen up, whoever's listening: we can't all be
Marcus Aurelius. Most of us are Alexanders, killing
those we love most with our addled righteousness
and the cuts of a thousand broken promises.

Which leaves us with final questions: can I make it
from here to the ice machine in just my underwear?
Or failing that, can someone change my checkout time?
More to the point: Can someone please call Melissa

and tell her this time I really mean it?

Swing

When jazz clarinetist Eric Dolphy died at age 37, many
critics assumed a drug overdose. But Dolphy never used drugs,
nor did he drink. He said on several occasions that he was
trying to imitate with his music the sound of birdsong.

With no light left in their wings,
blackbirds descend on the creek
to read their ill fortune in the rocks
while orioles fly back and forth
over the water, as if stringing
between the banks some invisible
Bridge of Sighs. In Venice, only
death waited on the other side
of those ramparts. These blackbirds
seem to understand. At times, even
I can see the girders and cables.
I think I know what it means
to be one's own executioner. I've
studied the instructions in a suicide
note my father didn't write.
When I hear the last plaintive strain
rise away from Eric Dolphy's
bass clarinet, I think of his early
death and then think of one final
breath leaving this hollow body.
In each courageous life, said my

favorite philosophers, there is
a right time to die. I know this isn't
it. Like I know it wasn't courage
that caused these broken wings.
But still I remember what Leo
said: to lose one's dignity is a fate
worse than death. That shame
is this creek bed where I wake
each morning with stones pressed
against my chest and bile pumping
through my blood. So yes, I can see
the vultures riding high thermals,
not as a symbol, but as a solid fact.
I meant what I said about broken
wings. I mean what I meant to say
about drinking from the clear spring
that rises under this ironwood tree.
Thank you, Eric Dolphy, for your solo
on *Serene*, for the way you urged us
blackbirds to shake these blues and
drop these rocks so we might at last
swing back inside your light.

Tanka (In Trouble)

i.

The purple hyacinth begins to bloom,
followed by a slope of forsythia.
A swallowtail romances a falling leaf.
Who bought you that old set of wings
I found in the attic?

ii.

One morning, my neighbor found a purple finch
still asleep on the edge of his feeder.
He cradled the tiny bird in one hand
and took it inside to show his sleeping wife.
But their marriage fell apart anyway.

iii.

It scared me that night
I walked into the dark living room
and saw you moving in step
with an invisible partner
because I refused to learn the tango.

iv.

Beside your bed lay a book called *Regret*,
but I thought it said *Egrets*,
and I remembered that line
by a lonely Chinese poet:
Only the egrets have understood me.

Across The Border

Once in Durango I watched a woman crawl, weeping,
from the entrance to the altar
of a great white church.

I felt like an impostor then,
thinking I would always be a tourist
in that land of grief.

Now, I feel quite native to such bewilderment,
quite at home here
on my knees.

Calling Cassiopeia

Gray with traffic dust,
        the scrubby geese walk single-file
                across the parking lot,

heading (if you can believe it)
        straight to the liquor store
                where a Mexican man

plays accordion for tips
        while his wife sells fajitas
                from her butane stove.

And I think, You web-footed fuckers.
        After all the poems I wrote
                about your impressive formations

in blue Kentucky skies,
        now you want to drag me back
                through this grim display

of dead cigarettes and spent lottery tickets?
        You want me to wait behind
                some jerk-off who's trying

to cash his daughter's McDonald's check,
        while his amped-up buddies huddle
                outside in a busted Corolla?

The owner tells the guy to get lost
        but he's happy to sell me a sack
                of half-pints that can't disguise

my own desperation.
        The man on accordion is playing
                "La Casa de Madera,"

as if to conjure the black clouds
        now sweeping down to erase even
                the shadow of myself.

Back in my old clapboard house,
        the woman I used to share it with
                is nowhere to be found.

Tonight's storm sounds like an intruder
        as it tries a thousand hands
                at my doors and windows.

The dying fire sleeps
        like an old dog too feeble
                to scare off this cold.

My pitched roof is the hull
        of an upturned ship that cuts furrows
                into the night sky

as it rides out this squall.
       Planks bulge and creak
              at their joints and rivets.

Submerged inside this solitude,
       I drift with my drink from
              room to room, like a clapper

trapped inside a diving bell.
       "Cassiopeia," I call out
              to my favorite constellation,

"Please don't leave me here alone.
       I'll bring you five sea-lilies
              and three pink starfish.

Just pull me out
       of this descending dark
              and point my astrolabe

to some city of light where
       grounded prayers might still get
              one last hearing."

Shock Corridors

1.

There was this guy in detox wearing *Star Wars* pajama
pants that he held up with one hand because the staff
had taken away all our drawstrings and shoe laces.
They even took away my watch, afraid I might pry off
its back and slit my wrists with the inner workings.
Or maybe they just thought time was irrelevant here.
They were right. We wandered through lockdown
with nowhere to go and no way to get there. We watched
counselors make lists on a white board of all the ways
to stay clean (take a walk, breathe deeply, chew ice), until
it was time once more to fight over the cigarette box.

2.

My roommate was a jockey who really loved meth
and had even loved his stepmother until he came to suspect
she had been plotting the World Trade Center attacks.
"Let's go to sleep and not think about that," I suggested.
He had another twenty-eight, court-ordered days to go here.
Said he used to shoot rats and heroin up at Saratoga.
Then, one day, he and his horse both failed their drug test.
"That's some karmic shit right there," he told me.
I said it was for a fact and then shut out the bedside light.

3.
We marched single-file, like inmates, to each meal.
Then orderlies ordered us back to our cinder block rooms.
We slept under thin blankets on hard beds, were awakened
every twenty minutes to make sure we hadn't died.
There were no windows, and yet I felt a painful flow
of traffic humming past the unit at all hours, drivers
oblivious to our damage, our cravings, our presence.
The world was unforgivably going on without us,
but we had been plucked from a life we could no longer
navigate and dropped into these shock corridors.
The only way out seemed too terrible to fathom.

4.
The nurse took our blood pressure four times a day,
asked about headaches and itching, said to hold out
our hands so she could monitor how badly they shook.
When I asked her when mine might finally steady,
she held up her own trembling right hand and said,
"I've been where you are now. Just go to meetings."
She treated us with such compassion; it was a kind
of grace really. We had all finally arrived at the last house
on the block, metaphorically speaking, and she listened
without judgment to our desperate justifications, our

ridiculous reimagining of the things we couldn't change.
I myself couldn't imagine what serenity might be,
but the nurse looked me in the eye when she spoke,
and she seemed in possession of the thing I needed most.
I thought of the bodhisattva who refuses enlightenment
until she has dragged the rest of us along with her
to the threshold of nirvana, to the end of thirst and fear.

5.

One night the *Star Wars* kid and I watched football on TV
while waiting for our last dose of phenobarbital.
He said he'd started for the state championship team
five years ago. The guy was impossibly emaciated.
"Did you play safety?" I asked. He looked offended
for a moment, then replied, "No, middle linebacker. But
that was before Afghanistan. And all the fucking drugs."
I nodded, then he turned straight toward me and said,
"You know what, though? I never hocked my ring.
Shit, basic training was nothing compared to summer
workouts. Our coaches were sadistic sons of bitches,
but we won the motherfucker. I've still got the ring."
He blew his nose on the sleeve of his shirt, then limped
over to where the pharmacist waited with our pills.

6.

"What do you do on the other side?" one of the orderlies
asked me. "I'm a teacher," I said. "I thought so," she replied.
"I've never seen anyone else read a book around here."
Really, I was just letting my sore eyes drift over
the same words: *Men have died from time to time,*
and worms have eaten them, but not for love.
The young woman looked at my slim paperback and said,
"Hey, you know what? I was Rosalind in that play

back in high school." "That's pretty cool," I said.
"Do you know what I remember?" she asked. "Tell me."
"Sweet are the uses of adversity." "Great line," I said.
"Ain't it?" She grinned, then quickly rose to break up
a violent argument one man was having with himself.

7.

"This is our last date," I joked with the nurse while she
took my blood pressure the night before I got discharged.
My vitals had slightly improved, my hands still shook.
She just smiled and said, "Go to meetings." The next morning,
I said goodbye to the jockey and the *Star Wars* kid.
They were busy at the wall phone, calling around for
a halfway house that might take them in. Neither could
believe I actually had someone, a wife no less, coming
to collect my sorry self. And when the jockey saw
Melissa waiting at the nurses' station, he looked
up at me and said, "Christ, man, don't fuck that up."
I shook his hand and assured him that I certainly would
not.

II

Narcissism

"A drinking man is a fading man," Leo said
on the day I emptied all the bottles in our house,
then ceremoniously drove them to the county dump,
where I flung each one from the bed of my truck
and then sat down on the tailgate to stare out into
the terrifying rest of my life. My hands shook.
My toes had gone numb and blood was leaking
out my asshole. Leo said that was to be expected.
Then he started quoting a Merle Haggard song.
That music had long been the soundtrack of my
life, and I knew how the right steel guitar could
hold a man hovering just above rock bottom.
I even once wrote a poem in homage to the Hag
that said vicarious misery is decent company,
but now I felt too alone even for that consolation.
I couldn't fathom all the days I'd have to stack
just to reach a place where life without booze
might be bearable, much less, as Leo promised,
desirable. What I desired that morning was a cold
pint of Tito's to wash down a Xanax or three.
Then I could stew for a while outside the liquor
store, with a fifth stashed under the jumper cables,
and figure out the rest of my day. There would be
lies to reenact, guardrails to circumvent, and
the contents of a mailbox to avoid at all costs. Or:
I could drive home and shake apart out in my shop.

Which is what I did. Tools rusting from neglect
hung in judgment above my workbench with
a contempt they made no effort to contain.
That's always how it is with inanimate objects.
Mirrors, of course, are the worst, which is why
I'd been avoiding them for months. The hatred they
conveyed seemed to well up from the curse that
Nemesis was happy to cast over idiot Narcissus.
I certainly didn't want to linger over reflections
of a bloodshot eyes and carbuncular skin. There
was no question this narcissist had seen better days,
had once even seen a world beyond himself.
But that world slowly narrowed to a chicken coop
where the hens and I could drink alone in peace,
even carving recriminations into plywood walls if
it came to that, and be assured it came to that.
But no one needs the Greek myths I learned in
middle school to understand this cold uncaring.
It had been on full display for quite some time.
I was too high to help when a neighbor called
about floodwater pouring into his basement.
I was too drunk to drive when Melissa's car
broke down on the interstate miles from town.
Even my sister's cancer was an abstract concern.
I just didn't sit well beside other people's hurt.
It was a full-time job manufacturing my own.
"There's a wind blowing through that hollow
place in your soul," Leo said, and I decided to
trust his diagnosis before it turned into autopsy.
I decided to wrap that cavity in chicken wire
until I could plaster something more substantial
in its place. That my promises meant nothing,
even I understood. The withering fig tree would

have to bear fruit or be culled by the Revelator's
justified scythe. That, to me, felt only fair.
Still there seemed time to revise the old myth.
In this new telling, Narcissus drives his truck
down to the river. But kneeling there on the bank,
he looks beneath his wavering reflection at darters
and dace fighting for their own endangered lives.
Hellgrammites hunt in the grass shadows.
Stone rollers nudge pebbles aside, perhaps
making way for some unlikely resurrection.
But Narcissus wants only to imagine that these
creatures are erasing his bloated, haggard face.
He wants to imagine his own features fading
into theirs, his own mangled self disappearing
downstream on a merciful wave of release.

Repairs

I used to hide out here in my shop with a bottle of vodka
and at least enough sense not to touch any power tools.
Now a coffee pot sits next to the drill press. Brewing,
it reminds me of August mornings in a Maine boatyard,
where we turned old plans into beautiful wooden poems.
I was building a bank dory that summer, based on the one
Henry and John Thoreau rowed from Concord, Mass. to

Concord, New Hampshire in the summer of 1840.
My boat had beautiful, low-slung lines and a narrow
tombstone transom. I painted the hull green with a blue
sheer plank to reflect, as Thoreau said, both river and sky.
That fall, a poet asked what I had done with my summer.
When I told her I built a small wooden boat, she smiled
and said softly, "Ah, that's what I see in your eyes."

The Thoreau brothers loaded their boat with melons;
I stowed under my thwarts a more fermented concoction
when I rowed Melissa all around Cave Run Lake, fishing
for muskie and drinking like Li Po under a full moon.
Then I let the boat molder for years under a gray tarp.
The gunwales started to splinter while the oarlocks rusted.
I drank away three summers I had promised repairs.

Now the neglected dory sits on sawhorses up in my shop.
Most fall weekends, I put on a pot of coffee, then get to work
patching rot in the planks and stiffening the transom.
I repaint the hull and slather the seats with spar varnish.
Come May, we will fish the quarry walls for bluegill.
Who knows? We might even go whaling with the clock hands
I stole from every blank face in every dive bar on earth.

The Art of Living

—for Jim and Chuck

1.

My fly line unspools across the water like a long sentence
whose final punctuation is a grizzly hackle tied by a friend.

He clamped his fly vise to the branch of a fallen pine
right after we arrived by mule train to this Montana river.

Bent over the dead branch, he wove silk and bucktail into
this imaginary insect that drifts like a stonefly on the current.

I snap the line out again, and this time, a cutthroat trout
dives with my fly down into a deep, emerald eddy.

The rod comes alive in my hand, and that right there is
the dopamine jolt I came all this way to feel, the narcotic

spark I haven't known since the day I put the bottle down.
The trout, with its almond-sized brain, must feel the same

when it rises to my fly and our neural streams converge.
That's how survival wired us for this great and brutal craving.

The other three anglers and I toss our gutted fish in flour,
then cook them over a flame that has always burned

beside this river and continues to scour these mountains.
Pink fireweed flowers all around the charred trees.

Mayflies couple in the air above us while swirling night-
hawks snatch them out of their own Mesozoic dreams.

2.

Gin-clear is how fishermen describe the tributaries
that flow into the Flathead River and send native trout
gliding through the turbulent boils of narrow gorges.

A river is always reinventing itself. The underworld's work
is done; now it's the water's turn to slowly carve apart
all this limestone and find its way north to Canadian lakes.

A large buck in full velvet leaps across a small feeder creek.
Preening mergansers cock their heads as I wade the shallows.
After days on the river, time starts to seem an urban artifact.

It doesn't cease to exist so much as it becomes irrelevant.
And once time drops away, all that's left is this moment,
stretching like its own kind of eternity. Here inside that
    pocket,

I can think only about my fly drifting on the current
and the cutts that might rise to take it. Here I can let my mind
bathe free in its absolute attention, this strange new chance

to re-inhabit my life. I watch another angler casting
beautiful loops downstream, and I wonder if all our days
could be conducted with such artistry, precision, and care?

3.

When the older fishermen retire to their tents, I stay up
and watch shooting stars arc just above pine silhouettes.

My desire for wilderness and clarity are coalescing here
in this million-acre backland where only animal energy—

the mules' and mine—was permitted to carry us this deep
into the dark. Grizzlies are feeding at higher altitudes

while Ursa Major lumbers even further overhead.
The entire night sky reaches down like a splattered dome

and at its apogee stands Gemini, my own duplicitous sign.
One star is the dead Siamese twin I'm trying to cut loose,

the other another self I might yet find the courage to become.
Lying is the first inclination of both anglers and drunks.

One wants a better story, and one wants to be left alone
with the only friend that understands this insatiable thirst.

A year ago, my hands shook so bad I could barely thread
my fly. This year I wrestled a bull trout to the river bank.

Translating Sappho While Listening To Billie Holiday

Your voice breaks
and Ulysses' sail rises
from deep inside the song.

Back home the hero still
has lipstick on his collar,

but you offer only bleak
resignation: "Don't Explain."

Even a god would stop
chasing some Daphne long enough
to listen to you,

who could slay any suitor
with that fragile song.

It gets under your skin,
burns there like dry grass,
like junk,

      like the hurt
you can't feel hard enough.

When I try to speak,
my tongue is only a cold coin
that could never pay
the ear's tribute.

Now the hollow instrument
lies quiet in its case.

But somewhere
in between living and dying,
your bruised heart escaped its cage

like a bluebird
wearing the whole sky
on its wings.

Christmas Letter to a Friend, Eight Years Sober

Dear Darcy,

All color has drained from these Kentucky woods.
My neighbor hangs Christmas lights on his cattle gate
each December, and it cheers me up a little. I passed on
egg nog at the grocery today because I couldn't imagine
it without whiskey. Maybe next year I'll feel different.
At a church down the street, cars lined up for a DRIVE-THRU
LIVE NATIVITY. I wish you had been here to see it, that
poor high school Mary, shivering inside a Home Depot barn,
cradling in her arms some Cabbage Patch son of man.
How did a gospel for the poor ever become this religion
of convenience, of families lined up in their Volvos?
The radio says someone stole a sculpture of Abe Lincoln's
hand from a museum in Kankakee. When aides complained
that Grant was a drunk, Lincoln supposedly replied,
"Tell me which whiskey he drinks, and I'll send it to all
my generals." It works until it doesn't, is what I've found.
Many thanks for driving up last month during my freak-out.
You make clean living look like the opposite of deprivation.
Melissa says I'm lucky to have you for a friend and it's true.
One drunk talking to another drunk seems all we understand.
You're right about the awful, early morning recriminations.
It's good now to wake without immediately thinking up

a lie or an apology. Last week, I got my sobriety date
etched into that old Zippo lighter. When I drive past
liquor stores, I reach for it in my pocket and say out loud,
'Eleven-twenty-seven,' like some kind of incantation.
So far, that seems to be working. I don't know how to pray
to something I can't believe in; still, every morning I read
a letter from Seneca to Lucilius. And I repeat the words
Leo told me to recite: 'Not today, alcohol. My self-respect
and dignity aren't for sale.' At first, I thought I only wanted
to quit drinking. Now, I see how each day might be an answer
to the question: How should I live? An answer that can only
mean some act that reaches beyond myself. I was sorry
to hear about Jo. She went down in a hard way. I found
an old picture of us all, a bunch of rebels without a clue
about the futures we'd abandon for booze. I hope one day
I can put all those wasted years to some use. As you have.

Wishing you peace in this season of possibility,

Erik

PS. Tell Lauren I said good luck with her folk art show.
If she needs more yarn, I'm thinking about raising alpacas.
Melissa says that's fine if it keeps me out of the bars.
I hear her singing softly in the mornings now as she gets
ready for work, something she never did when I drank.
It's almost enough to make a man believe in God. Almost.

Water Tower Manifesto

In another time it would have been
a beer on this back road,

wind whipping your hair
and the radio blasting Big Star.

Today it's just me at the wheel
and a kestrel on the wire.

Up on the swells,
Charolais cows look like clouds,

and I think:
I'd like to paint that

if I could, but I can't.
So I decide that my eye

is its own camera
and my mind

the emulsion where
those white cows

get transformed
into a higher art,

a lens through which
the world passes

back into its own
neglected intensity.

"There is another world
and this is it," said Eluard.

I'm feeling good.
I won't deny it.

I'm thinking some sky-
high thoughts, like that

eternity is a trap door
inside each passing moment,

and each earthly body
is some version

of the whole
and the holy.

I know I'm not the first
to say any of that,

but who ever really was?
And who now is climbing

this long narrow ladder
with a can of Krylon

in his back pocket,
rising high above the tree line,

risking life and limb
to publish this poem

on the side of the county
water tower?

It's me, that's who:
the container of solitudes,

the last man out
of Shakytown,

the ancient astrolabe
that still bears on its back

the gold tooling
of an unfinished universe.

The Panther

The day our Sobriety Camp ended, the Circus Camp came to town. Out on the village green, the shift in tone was disconcerting. While a few former drunks (hopefully former drunks) huddled together, weeping softly, whispering words of mutual affirmation, two excitable teenagers started to juggle small chairs. After every fourth rotation, each juggler jettisoned one part of his ensemble over to the other, while both continued to keep all of their furniture aloft. It was impressive. The drunks even said so. But they still seemed too dazed by their new life to really get in on the act. It was different with the clowns, who of course seemed sad—carrying around, as they do, the world's nervous laughter. We drunks understood about high wires, too, having tried all manner of balancing acts to waver above that awful finality called Rock Bottom. Still, when the tightrope walker cinched her taut stage between two trees, we marveled at her poise, how she could recite the alphabet backward while standing on one leg, the other tucked up behind her head. But then, we reasoned, she wasn't staring into a Maglite on the side of a dark road, while some silhouette officer barked impossible instructions. Of course, we all broke into foolish tears when the magician produced three white doves from under his dark foulard. After that, our families arrived to gather up whatever was left of us. "You're here, you're here," I susurrated to Melissa, half in disbelief, half in boundless gratitude. Her eyes were so kind and full of pity—neither of us noticed when the lion tamer quietly lifted a sleek black panther into the trunk of our car.

Gethsemani

As the bells pealed for vespers, I was
thinking that a monk possesses a pond
in as much as the pond possesses a monk.
Such is his kingdom's only economy.

"The gates of heaven are everywhere,"
wrote the monk who wore his barn jacket
like a vestment, with notebooks and poetry
tucked in the large denim pockets.

His face seemed that of a man who had
never looked in a mirror. So I set fire to
all of my own empty masks and sent that
flotilla out across the small dark pond.

Shaker Dreams

We should do everything as if we had a thousand years to live
and as if we were going to die tomorrow.

—MOTHER ANN LEE

Down below the western slope, where saxifrage
blooms along the outcrops, a spring comes to life
beneath the forked roots of an ancient sycamore.
What can one make of all these daily resurrections,
these miracles that seem as common as caddis flies?
Seneca wrote of the forest's lofty dignity and said
we should worship at the source of great rivers.
I think he might have been right about that.
My own river crawls to light in the Cumberlands,
among blasted mountains and long-abandoned stills.
Acid leaks orange from old mines, while a hundred
miles downstream, I walk beside the poison waters
of this crumbling republic. But once at a landing down
the road, a small group of Shakers loaded flatboats with
butter and hemp bound for Natchez and New Orleans.
Further up on these meadowlands, those true believers
got down to the business of building paradise on earth.
Work was their constant prayer, and they held all
things in common, as the Book of Acts decreed.
Their village had everything but banks and jails.
They took in fugitive slaves and runaway brides,
bred long-horn bulls and invented the clothespin.

They engineered their own salvation in the kingdom
of God, which happened to be a farm in Kentucky.
Today the believers' last surviving bull drowses in
the shade of a bur oak, while I wander the ruins of
Eden, high above the river that brought a self-chosen
people here. But it wasn't the impossibility of their
vision that sacked the Shakers. That's just what
we tell ourselves to justify these compromised lives.
No, it was Confederate hooligans and industrial
dreams that razed this place called Pleasant Hill,
birthed upon a nation the ugliness that remains
our true inheritance. Down at Shaker Landing,
I crank to life the motor of my own small boat
and head back downstream, past a heron rookery
that looks to me now like its own timeless utopia.
I myself am learning by the day how to live in such
an animal present, where the past can't bind me
and what's to come doesn't look so daunting.
It's been seven months since I last had a drink.
When I pass under the herons' raucous colony,
one regal blue sets off from its crowded nest
and glides down the river as if leading me home.

Hypaethral

Watching two fawns follow a doe across Clear Creek,
or watching a queen snake swallow a sunfish
is about as close to God as I can get.

The sanctuary of my grandfather's church had white plaster
  walls
and over the baptistery a Jesus who looked like he came from
  New Jersey.

My grandfather's hard-shell faith hung like a noose over my
  father's head.
My grandmother demanded an open casket as if to say the
  bullet missed.

As if to say her God approved.
As if to say her God existed.

My mother raised me by herself in rural Virginia.
Every morning, she poached an egg for each of us in tiny
  brown bowls.
Then she went to her teaching job
and I hid in a large cardboard box at the babysitter's house.

Years later, I stopped burying my head in the stars of heaven.
Now I've whittled my own metaphysics down to this:

We can say the world is wholly material,
or we can say the world is wholly divine—

and each means exactly the same.

Now I'm perched on this limestone rim,
surrounded by a congregation of chinquapin oaks.
If I sit here long enough, star-bellied spiders will bind me to
    the trees
with their own natural philosophy, spelled out in silver
    filament.

After Attar's tireless flock of birds
passed through the seven valleys of tribulation,
they asked to finally see their god.
But all they saw was their own reflections.
And at once they understood.
The whole journey had been worth that.

After my grandfather passed, I moved my membership
to this unroofed church in Woodford County, Kentucky,
where I now bow down to hepatica and wild iris,

where I now fold short odes into paper boats
that disappear over the falls,
beyond a blind horizon.

The Rising

1.

I am trying to distill my one life
down to some essential objects:
my grandfather's silver lighter,
a book of poems by Paul Celan,
this handsome fly rod that whips
like a willow branch in the wind.

2.

These are things that might ground
an otherwise flailing man, set him
down beside a wide Montana river
where the cutthroat are forgiving
and he can fish all day under clouds
the size of small island nations.

3.

My grandfather taught me to handle
a lake canoe, but he never said how
I might pick up my father's lost trail.
I searched one winter for the solitary
wolverine, but all I found in the snow
was an alphabet of indifference. Still,

4.
I'd like to think a tree-high thought,
as Paul Celan once wrote in despair.
I'd like to lie down in the shade of that
thought. I'd like to watch that thought
wing its way over to the other side of
fear, where trout are said to be rising.

Good Again

Does a god always dream itself into being,
or is that us dreaming the god dreaming ourselves,
like two facing mirrors, endlessly inventing one another?

An artist ground together rose petals and moth wings,
then pressed the fragments between strips of celluloid
so we might watch them bleed across the screen
or flutter behind our eyes.

But long before those dream machines,
we painted images on the inside of our skulls,
then cast them out onto cave walls:
black reindeer, ocher bison, red aurochs.

We were never that good again.

Some say those early artists blew their colors onto the cave
     walls
through hollow griffin bones.
Some say those early artists bore five holes in a griffin bone
and breathed into it the first music.

The self, I like to think, can ride the breath out of the body.
Where it goes is another question.

But I do know this about those early *Homo sapiens*—
they wanted to be more than what we are.
They wanted to ride far beyond the borders of this flesh.

We were never that good again.

Sitting in his Small Garden, the Reclusive Socialist Ponders The Teachings of Epicurus

July is the month he loves most
here in this karst country.

The reclusive socialist prepares
for his less reclusive wife
a dinner from their garden:

tomatoes, beans, cucumbers, okra.

Afterward, he sits in a canvas chair
among his raised beds
and reads Epicurus, who wrote:

"Everything easy to procure
is natural.
Everything difficult to obtain
            is superfluous."

Thus, the study of nature
would make us modest
and self-sufficient.

If only it were so,
thinks the reclusive socialist,

who is himself
no measure of modesty.

But sitting beneath sunflowers,
their heavy, spent heads drooping
like shepherd's staffs
while the waxing moon rises
over hackberry trees,

he feels his afflictions dissipate
into an unexpected calm.

He feels his failures decompose
into a useful humus.

He feels the philosopher's ancient hand
finally come to rest
on his shoulder.

That Which Is

A stone Buddha sits in the tile hearth
where gas logs once burned to warm this old house.

The Buddha gives off no heat.
He is cold down to his stony heart, which is not a heart at all
but only this dense collection of molecules,
too crowded to ever house the soul

                              or even a sacred spark
                              to set the world afire.

This Buddha is no savior.
In his stillness he promises nothing.
You cannot hang him from a cross.
You cannot feast on his symbolic flesh.

You might heave him from a ledge high above an ancient
    gorge,
but he would only tumble down to the streambed,
knocking against other stones until he came to rest

among the headwaters
that for millions of years smoothed his shoulders
into this deep calm

and taught him the sermon
that the stone Buddha now preaches
in silence
from our hearth.

Circles

*Our life is an apprenticeship to the truth that around every circle
another can be drawn . . .*

—EMERSON

We come together in circles,
though some chairs always sit empty as missing teeth.

Stories move around the room:
the one about a child you can't get back,
the one about a stolen .38 and a change of clothes in a red
    bowling bag
("And I don't even bowl . . .")

—stories handled so often, they wear the sheen of anonymity.

The eye's cornea and the moon's Humboldt Crater.
The peacock's tail and the spiral nebula.
The bell of Eric Dolphy's clarinet drinking in the sun.

"God," said at least one saint, "is a center without a
    circumference."
"The saint," said at least one god, "contains multitudes."

I open my laptop to gaze at an image of the blue-green Earth
as seen from space, and my breathing begins to calm.
Dendrochronology, I recently learned, is the study of tree rings.
Drought years. Mast years.
Catastrophe. Rebirth.

A fire ring on the Cumberland Plateau stares up into the night
   sky.

Stories move around the fire,
the one about crashing drunk through a glass table,
the one about pissing in the oven when you thought it was the
   john.
Every mountain is a blue sail riding the horizon.

Like a three-legged dog, I return to circle the wolf trap,
searching for my phantom limb,
searching for what I can't get back.

Homecoming

We woke beside the river,
then shed dead skins for
the kingfishers to find.
The current moves among
white limestone bluffs
like blood among bone,
like a thread leading out of
the self's dark labyrinth,
like a god reinventing itself
in every moment, a god
always and never the same.
What we see in the river,
said all the rustic mystics,
is the face we wore
before we were born,
the name we were given
before our given name.
Orpheus called the oaks
down from the mountains
so Jason could carve from
their hearts the *Argo*'s keel.
I press my backbone against
the stone creek bottom and
let its water wash over me.
I am a skin boat now,
ribs rising among sunfish,
arms reaching for departure.

The Kingdom of God

This creek is a good companion, I think,
walking a narrow bank path cut by the deer.

October light filters through trees and lands
like gold leaves on the water. We might

have inherited a god of such sunlight, were
it not for dark Golgotha and this chronic urge

to drink blood from sacrificial lambs.
All these human fears seemed to crave such

strange justifications from our man-god.
Once dead, he could get down to the real work

of drinking in our own pain so we wouldn't have to.
But if I read the Gospels right, all the man-god

really wanted was walk the beautiful earth,
calling attention to the heaven we might find

at our feet if we could only stop
enumerating our sins and inventing infernos.

Alas, we didn't listen. We like our streets
running with blood, our schoolchildren's flesh

flailed from their bodies. And after registering
the usual, unastonished astonishment at this

version of Christendom, we sigh, shake
our heads, and say, "Now, who needs a drink?"

Joanie

I waited in my old Impala outside your father's strip club
and watched the great neon tiger beat its orange tail
against a huge martini glass. Inside at the bar, you
dropped a lit match into a coffee can full of receipts,
then brought out a fifth of well whiskey. The cruel girls
back in school called you a slut by association; the boys
suggested you grind on the tetherball pole at recess. But
after graduation, you and I beat those back roads down,
passing the bottle, passing the cornfield abortion signs,
passing between us a silence we thought pregnant with
articulation, pregnant with a language so precise the words
would stun us when they finally came, which they never
did. Here in this old deck chair, I can almost summon
the ardor I felt about your tight sweater, the mystery
of mysteries rising beneath it. I'm sorry I never answered
those long, perfumed letters. Your brothers scared me.
Your father seemed destined for the pen. I didn't understand
how you could navigate with such lightness all of that
claustrophobic masculinity. I realized too late you hoped
I might help, since I had a car and a book of poems.
Who was it? Dylan Thomas? John Berryman? You thought
my father's suicide had prepared me for a compassion
that would unfold once resentment burned away. Maybe
it did, but that was still decades off, after rock bottom
and rehab. I'm sure all your letters disappeared in boxes
full of cross-country trophies and bad shop projects.

I wish now I had laminated one of your poems to
a beveled piece of oak, but that's a sentimental notion
you would have laughed at as you reached for the bottle
and wedged it between your thighs. Those old cornfields
would have disappeared, with the river just over the rise.

Escape Velocity

In another life I'd like to come back as a string quartet,
or at least a man who can stop after two drinks.

Inconceivable really that my body's every cell already knew
    its fate.

Still we must believe in free will, said some joker,
because we have no other choice.

The nurse drew blood with my Osprey fountain pen
so I could write this down and be done with it.
Except I'm never done with it.

                                As the blood left my vein
I stared out the window
and watched a grand piano beat against the horizon with its
    one black wing.

That was me lurching from day to day
like a dodo failing to achieve escape velocity.

But I did escape extinction. At least for now,
and the now is where I reside on my best days.

"Praise the gods," said Marcus.
"Do good to others."

Everything else is ash and bleached bones,

and if one acquires a name, it's only sound and echo
sound and echo.

Second Life

The rope burns on my wrists

are not as sinister

as they look.

I was only trying to lasso

the trunk of a fallen ash tree

and pull it off the bent bough

of a still living oak.

Flight

1.

A man next to me on the midnight plane
from Chicago to Lexington spent the hour
writing a spidery note on thin blue paper

that he folded into a small origami bird. When
we disembarked, the man handed his creation
to the flight attendant in a fetching black skirt

and told her he'd be waiting at baggage claim.
Does such anonymous seduction ever work?
While I admire the brass, I really wouldn't know.

2.

All my life has been a long series of flights
from women, potential friends, anyone else
that might draw me out into the arc of failure.

Fear, someone told me after a meeting, is
an acronym for *Fuck everything and run*.
To tell the truth, that explains quite a lot

about all those nights I sprinted through
serpentine alleys of the hippocampus,
desperate for any bar that might still be open.

3.
Now booze no longer fuels my aspirations.
When there's nothing left to go on, just go
on your nerve, counseled Frank O'Hara.

Maybe that's the opposite on fear: to go
on what burns in your blood after you locked
all the trap doors of chemical retreat. Maybe

that's when you start looking people in the eye,
and just feel good outside the airport terminal
as the cool night brushes up against your skin.

Deus Absconditis

Absence is the form God takes in this world.

—SIMONE WEIL

I always thought that would be a great band name,
the Absconding Gods. They would be one of those
legendary acts that everybody talks about, but no one
has ever actually seen. A band that books no dates,
sells no tickets, but has been known to perform in
underground ossuaries and abandoned paint factories.
Their music would only exist on old cassette tapes
that furtive acolytes pass on to the deserving few
like samizdat poems from the Polish Resistance.
Gods, I tend to think, are like that—haunting, elusive,
forever unfound. But who is this Higher Power that
always comes wrapped in the gauzy language of faith?
Why can't the incarnation just be this slope covered in
twin leaf and toothwort? Or the embryonic tree hiding
inside a walnut husk. The interventionist god I keep
hearing about seems more like the invention of those
who couldn't live inside uncertainty on this small,
far-flung planet. In frustration, I once told a man
at a meeting, "If your god didn't save six million Jews,
I doubt he cares too much about my drinking problem."
I'm afraid I prefer a god always hiding in plain sight,

a god of twin leaf and toothwort and the walnut tree,
a god folded into the selections of some great jukebox
in a bright, empty diner on a dark mountain road—
a presence lurking in the one place we forgot to look.

ıxie Highway Improv

I might be listening to Ann Magnuson sing "White Rental Car Blues," or I might just be driving through that song here on Atlantic Avenue at one a.m., with the humid coastal air swirling through open windows of this airport rental as I sail across Dixie Highway, which, were I to follow it north, would eventually lead me home to Louisville, back to a power plant beside the Ohio River, where I worked as a janitor, sweeping up fly ash on the long, infernal landings, before punching out to drink in a redneck bar called A1A because the owner fancied himself a Floridian of the Jimmy Buffet stripe, serving up weak cocktails in his parrot-and-palm tree shirts, wearing us out with his unctuous talk and yacht rock juke box, while we slumped over our drinks, still covered in the black grime of the plant, about as far from any island paradise as a man can get, a man who thirty years later would find himself drifting alone along cross streets that bind those two, epic arteries like strands linking a double helix, wrapped around my brain stem and pulsing with the A1 allele, which taxied me right into detox along its own dopamine highways with hourly tolls and no sign of an off ramp, if you, coterminous reader, in the spirit of the holidays, will allow these franchised metaphors to belabor themselves a little longer, since they do shoulder up beside real, now empty streets lined with cheerful neon signs and Christmas light strung up the trunks of palm trees and along the gunwales of pleasure boats that line the intercoastal, where I sit and wait for a drawbridge to rise so the rich can glide quietly through, while at an all-night diner, with its inviting yellow bricks and painted red mortar, I grab two crullers and a coffee to go, to go anywhere that isn't the hotel bar or a trap house, to go sailing over the breakers in a parachute harness or riding the back of a pelican, not the flight of a fugitive trying to outrun lies and liability, but rather the buoyancy of castaway padding his own pine box over the swells and under the beam from a lighthouse, perched at the inlet like a third-eyed obelisk that looks simultaneously inside and out, redirecting misguided alleles, sweeping the horizon with purpose.

Sous les Pavés, la Plage!

I love this low slant of light as it
sweeps over the tall grass at dusk.
A raven lazes across the sky while
doves swirl around wild grapevines.

Once we were born from oaks.
Isn't that the way Virgil tells it?
That's how I'd like to belong to
the world. I want to climb inside

the kingfisher's mind and lay my head
on a bed of fishbones. Or dive down
inside the beaver's lodge and drink
deep from the red October moon.

Under paving stones, the beach!
as the revolutionaries used to say.
There's something still worth fighting
for, in other words, and it's everything

we seem determined to bury beneath
the blueprints of our own demise—
everything that might mean redemption
back into the ancestral grove of oaks.

I suspect those trees are all we have

left, now that the god of forgiveness is
finished, offering only as little mercy
as we ourselves could manage.

I gaze down the river from this rock
and put my faith in the kingfisher,
a bird that always flies with a secret
treatise printed beneath its wings.

What I Learned From Marcus Aurelius

1. The body of Zeus is distributed equally throughout existence.

2. Live for your fellow if you want to live for yourself.

3. It pays to have a kind stepfather.

4. What's wanted is freedom of spirit for the individual, justice for the community.

5. Nature made us kin.

6. Turn inward so you can then turn outward.

7. The *self* is a verb, not a noun.

8. Justice, wisdom, courage, temperance.

9. Beware of plagues brought back from Parthian wars.

10. Some people obtain fame while others deserve it.

11. The philosopher should sleep on a hard cot with a simple animal skin.

12. The soul is always in league with the Whole.

13. The holy is everything we find and infuse.

14. You control your actions; fate controls the outcome.

15. If someone speaks ill of you, smile and say, "He was clearly unaware of all my greater faults."

16. Always take a book with you to the Colosseum.

17. The *daimon* is a god that can fit in your pocket.

18. To be truly free, seek not what is under others' control.

19. God and Nature are two names for the same single organism.

20. The value of failure is learning.

21. We must live deep in the imagination of the Earth.

22. Philosophy is a full-time mistress (especially if your wife is screwing half the Roman Senate).

23. Practice this: pessimism of the mind, optimism of the will.

24. Empire is an insatiable mouth devouring the earth.

25. The trick is: to at once abandon and invent the self.

26. No action should be taken without affirming the art of life.

27. Think of the world as one living creature, comprising one substance and one soul.

28. We are all temporal embodiments of the Whole.

29. Jettison judgment and you are saved.

30. Trust only the god that lives inside you.

Animals At Full Moon

Tonight the full moon is ringed with an iridescent glow.
Animals gather in the silver grass,
drawn into a ritual we no longer understand.

Down the street at the state hospital,
inmates spin wire cocoons out of their own mad love.

Those of us who don't sleep tied to our beds
turn restlessly between our sheets,
like eels rolling alone inside dark waves

because once we gathered around a fire under a full moon,
drawn into a ritual we no longer understand.

ontana Sketch

—*in the Bob Marshall Wilderness*

Morning fog settles into the saddles
of these hazy blue mountains.
I sit on a high cutbank and watch

the river kink around cottonwoods,
writing on rocks the latest entry
of its endless autobiography.

Gray veins that thread through
black volcanic rocks look like
bulbous maps of these braided streams.

A tough white flower called
the Grass of Parnassus muscles in
among the scree and scramble.

Clacking, careening grasshoppers
flash their yellow legs in dry sedge
before landing like small, dead leaves

no bird would ever disturb.
We try to fit words to our findings
and always fall short. Still, we try.

"You seem like a restless spirit,"
said a woman who had only known
me for three confounding hours.

I was doing my best Li Po impression,
getting determinedly drunk so I could
write some wild-grass calligraphy

and maybe drown embracing the moon.
I don't do that kind of thing anymore.
Now I'm just stacking twenty-fours,

staying clear of liquor stores,
and drinking at the springs that
arise inside these mountain spurs.

If I crawl through enough thickets
of red ozier and rabbitbrush, perhaps
I'll discover the river's source

and then start my whole story over.
'If you can't believe in God, just bow
down at any altar of unhewn stone,'

the voices in my head. Now I watch
a crossbill tear open a pine cone, then
pass each seed to his waiting mate.

Attitude of Gratitude

The green knives of irises pierce through the March snow.
A tiny pond has frozen in the hollow of a creek stone.
Flames in the woodstove run like fingers along a flute.
Osage wood burns hottest; osage fruit keeps mice away.
One woman at a meeting says, "Well, this New Year's Eve
I didn't put a gun in my mouth." Another adds, "I stopped
worrying what time my husband would come home. Or if
he ever would." At my feet, our dog shudders in his sleep.
From the rimrock, I watch two hawks circling at eye level.
A friend sends a poem in which he thanks the man who
flung three tires into his creek for not flinging the fourth.
After days of gray, sunlight spreads over the frosted grass.
Oaks again write their shadows down this western slope.
I slice kohlrabi and apples from the local orchard into
matchsticks, then mix them with salt, oil, and vinegar.
"To be one on whom nothing is lost," said Henry James.
What gratitude that would evoke. In a blue-gray dawn,
sandhill cranes fly between bullets and birdshot to find this
January cornfield. They leap into a spastic mating dance.
With mystical sleekness, otters dive over one another
in the deeper stretches of our creek, then ride the current
back to the river. Soaking in this old claw-foot tub, I feel
the pleasure of spent muscles after days of splitting wood.
Astronauts say that if we all saw the Earth from space, it
would seem worth saving. We would want to come home.

Mast Year

Morning in a mast year:
A gauzy fog hangs
in the fruit-heavy branches
of our walnut trees.

Down by the mailboxes
a doe grooms her fawn,
long tongue smoothing
back a white twitching ear.

The caterpillars roll up
inside oak leaves, then
bind them with a shroud
of silk. Such care.

It's the silence of these
trees that speaks for me.
A woods without words
is the poem I aspire to.

So yes, I've been thinking
lately of God as a verb,
as something moving
through the world and me,

not with any deliberation
or intent, but more like
a mirror idly studying
its own reflection.

Heliotropes

A song begins to form
inside the heart's dark abattoir,
                    then it slips out to climb the ladder of
                    my rib cage,
        searching for the double-syrinx of a local wood thrush.

        I was night gardening in my okra patch
when I looked up at Orion tangled once again in the branches
    of our hackberry tree
                    and thought: what use is all this loss
                            except to furrow the aboriginal soil
                            of the soul?

        In the morning, I watched the heliotrope follow its god
        across the sky.
The flower is a gnomon with no shadow,
                    an acolyte without a cause.
                In this way the heliotrope's prayer is never a
                plea,
                    only an act of praise.

        I too lean toward the sun, until my forehead
        touches
this earth, where bones have been ground down
                    and the flood-bent bloodroot presses its
                    face
                        against white limestone.

We are both supplicants
   at the mercy of strong currents,
      both practiced

   in the ways
   of early death

   and sometimes
   resurrection.

Acknowledgments

Some of these poems have appeared in the following journals:

Bangalore Review: "Shaker Dreams"
Brilliant Corners: "Myself When I Am Real" and "Swing"
Merton Seasonal: "Gethsemani" under the title "Monks Pond"
The Sun: "The Art of Living"
William and Mary Review: "Deus Absconditis"

The following poems appeared in two limited edition, letter-press chapbooks, set by Gray Zeitz at Larkspur Press:

A Short History of the Present: "Translating Sappho While
Listening to Billie Holiday" and "Tanka (in Trouble)"
Animals at Full Moon: "Animals at Full Moon," "That Which
Is," "Across the Border," and "Watertower Manifesto"

About the Author

 Erik Reece is the author of six books of nonfiction, including *Clear Creek, Utopia Drive,* and *Lost Mountain,* which won Columbia University's John B. Oakes Award for Environmental Journalism and the Sierra Club's David Brower Award for Excellence in Environmental Writing. His work has appeared in *Harper's,* the *Oxford American,* the *Atlantic, Orion,* and other publications. His two previous collections of poetry, *A Short History of the Present* and *Animals at Full Moon,* were published by Larkspur Press. He teaches writing and literature at the University of Kentucky and is the founder of Kentucky Writers and Artists for Reforestation.